Practical Prayer
for
Real Results

Rev. Bill Marchiony

PRACTICAL PRAYER FOR REAL RESULTS

Copyright © 2012 by Bill Marchiony

Published by Marchiony Consulting Partners LLC
137 Barrie Rd.
Ardmore, PA 19003

www.be-the-light.com

Additional copies of this book are available from
the publisher or through amazon.com.

Cover design by Dave Schpok
Edited by Donna Morrissey
Prayers edited by Rev. Joanne McFadden

All rights reserved. No part of this book may be used or reproduced by any means, graphical, electronic or mechanical including photocopying, recording, taping or by any information storage retrieval system without the written permission of the publisher except in the case of brief quotations embodied in critical articles or reviews.

ISBN: 1-477561-67-6
ISBN-13: 978-1477561676

Your new life
begins with a new thought.

PRACTICAL PRAYER FOR REAL RESULTS

Contents

Introduction 1

Using this Book 5

Prayers for Physical Wellness 14

Prayers for Emotional Wholeness 20

Prayers for Financial Prosperity 28

Prayers for Perfect Work & Creativity 32

Prayers of Spirit 38

Authority and Accountability 57

Praying for others 59

Scientific Prayer 61

Conclusion 65

Appendix – The Steps of Practical Prayer explained 69

DEDICATION

It's easy to see the path that is God's plan for our life. We just look over our shoulder at the footprints that have led to the present moment, and those steps are the path of God. We usually have a range of choices about the next step we take, and the only thing that's certain is that whatever we choose, our next step, too, is the path of God.

I have been blessed by a life path of joys and growth opportunities. They've all been good, even though many of the growth opportunities didn't seem so wonderful at the time.

This book is dedicated to the people and influences that have brought me to this present moment – able to write a book about Practical Prayer. In the years I spent as an overly intellectual head-based agnostic, this would have seemed pretty improbable. The thanks go to Karen Vedrode, the counselor whose tough love got me to look at the "me" within. I also thank all of the teachers and ministers and prayer partners who have been with me on the path.

Special gratitude to my prayer partner, Rev. John Hannes, and to Mike Savarese and Dave Kro, who have been part of a weekly Mastermind group that's kept me accountable for my consciousness for the past eight years. Also to the dozens of teens and Teen Advisors who have helped me put into perspective and come to peace with the beliefs I acquired as a teenager. Dr. Joanna Carmichael opened her heart and the Kalyana Centre to create a beautiful space for me to bring these ideas to print. Rev. Joannne McFadden has been an anchor, ready to remind me of Principle at the times that my ego has tried to grab control. Thanks to Donna Morrissey, a gifted editor who shared her exceptional talents and her deep Catholic faith to bring perspective and insight to this project and order to my chaos of commas.

A great big thank you to Rev. Dave Schpok, co-founder of New Thought Philadelphia, for his repeated reminders about consciousness and Law and his persistent willingness to point out when my personal Belief System is blocking the Light.

Deepest gratitude to my wife Dena, who saw the power and presence of my spiritual nature long before I even acknowledged that it existed and who, through inspiration and exasperation, has been with me through every step.

Practical Prayer for Real Results

Introduction

Prayer works. It has been part of the fabric of many people's lives for thousands of years and in many cases, people report miraculous results. The process described in this book is anchored in the rich history of prayer, free of the dogma and personality of any particular religion or belief system.

A Practical Prayer is a prayer that is answered. Pray for unexpected income and find a $20 bill lying on the ground. Or get a new job. Pray for a loving relationship and meet someone wonderful. Or fall in love again with the person you married. Pray for safety and security for a loved one and find out the police just happen to be setting up a community outreach center on their block. You get the idea.

Practical Prayer is a clearly defined sequence of steps intended to bring something new to the life or experience of the person doing the prayer. The formula was distilled from a common thread found in the spiritual practices of religions and disciplines all over the world. Practical Prayer is based on spiritual mind treatment, created by Dr. Ernest Holmes. He did his work in the early part of the 20th century and established Religious Science.

The process is scientific because it has been proven to work for anyone, regardless of his or her religion, race, gender, location, financial position, history, etc. Practical Prayer was developed and proven using the scientific method to the greatest extent possible in creating repeatable experiments in a context that is inherently subjective.

Practical Prayer for Real Results

"It is done unto you as you believe," "we create our own experience," "change your thinking, change your life," and the Law of Attraction all mean the same thing. Practical Prayer is a technique that enlightened Masters have used throughout history. There's a familiar example spoken by Jesus, which is included at the end of the prayer section. Practical Prayer allows anyone to change their beliefs and bring about a change in their life experience.

There are five steps in a Practical Prayer, which we'll explore in detail. Many practitioners add two more steps when they experience doubt about the truth of their affirmation. Some can do it – sometimes – in a single step. In this introductory book, we'll focus on the longer five and seven step versions.

Each Practical Prayer in this book is complete. You can read them in any order, once or repeatedly, silently to yourself or shouted from a mountaintop. Most have a blank line where you can insert specific results that you'd personally like to experience in your life. When you're inserting your own requests and desires, there are three important aspects to the language you use: make it positive, life affirming, and in the present tense.

Most importantly, this is a learning tool. It is intended to help you get started doing Practical Prayer. Once you are comfortable with the formula, you'll be making them up yourself. These are short, especially when compared to lengthy prayers with flowery language sometimes done by ministers or professionally trained practitioners at public gatherings. Remember, there is no magic to the specific words. It is your beliefs – your thoughts backed up by your feelings – which change your life.

Introduction

Love and Law

The philosophy behind Practical Prayer runs through many of the world's religions and spiritual practices. In a nutshell, it is the concept that everything is created by a single power and that everything in Creation follows the same natural laws.

It doesn't matter whether you think of the Creator as God in the book of Genesis, or as the organizing force that caused the Big Bang, or any other Creation story. Before there was the Universe that we live in, there was Some Thing, and It had an idea or in some way put Its creative energy into action. It created everything and continues to do so.

Painters, writers, and artists of all sorts know that deeply creative acts are a sharing of their inner energy – expressions of Love. The creative act that brought our Universe into being could be no less; leaving us with the certain understanding that the entire Universe in which we live is a creation of Love.

The Laws of Nature are unchanging. They work the same way now as they did thousands of years ago. The only thing that changes is our understanding of them and how to work with them. The laws of aerodynamics were not invented by the Wright Brothers. These two men were simply the first to understand them and apply them in a way that made it possible for people to fly. The principles were always there, and once humanity gained an understanding of them, it became possible for lots of people to build and fly airplanes.

The same is true of the creative laws of mind and spirit. When we apply the principles that have been used to create everything since the beginning of time, we activate the Law and get the same effect. As we become more deeply aware of the process of creation and the ways that the Law works, we are more fully able to create the experience we desire. The Law isn't changing or somehow working better. The Law is the Law and It responds in exactly the same way for everyone, at every time.

Your life – right now – is the result of all your beliefs, whether they've been the result of conscious action, childhood conditioning, or are part of the fabric of common beliefs that has evolved along with our civilization. Those beliefs are impressed into the Law, which creates the experience of your life. The good news is, you can change your beliefs and change your life.

"New Thought" is based on the notion that our lives are created by our thoughts or beliefs. Have a new thought and you create a new experience. This book is about creating new thoughts, and thereby creating new and preferable experiences. These forty Practical Prayers are each keyed to a particular theme. Each is complete, using either five or seven steps to assist you in changing a false or limiting belief into a new, more wholesome belief.

Using This Book

Believe It

A Practical Prayer need not be repeated or held in the mind for some period of time in order to be effective. This is a specific formula that allows the one praying to create a new belief, which is immediately reflected in the outer world of experience. There is no delay or time interval required between the moment a new belief is established in the mind and the change in circumstances.

I recall a time when I was in the middle of a tropical rainstorm, driving on the interstate. I was new to the process of affirmative prayer and set an intention for perfect weather. The rain stopped *instantly*[*]. I believed that it could, I accepted that whatever happened would be perfect, and the change in my outer experience was immediate.

Statements we make that don't reach the inner level of a belief will not change our experience so quickly or so profoundly. This is both good news and bad news. It's good, because we can be comfortable that not every passing thought or idea is going to come into our experience. Just imagine the life expectancy of a sports referee if it did! It's bad because sometimes we really want something to change, and it doesn't because deep inside we still have some hidden belief about it.

There is no reason to repeat a prayer and no reason not to. When you are guided to repeat one of these prayers, follow your

---

[*] In actuality, the rain didn't stop. It kept going wherever it is that rain goes when it's not raining on me. I wasn't controlling the weather. I was simply aligning myself with my perfect experience of the weather.

guidance. Furthermore, use it as insight to understand that there could be something in your belief system that's standing between you and whatever it is that you desire. In actuality, we never repeat a prayer. Even if you do it twice in a row, you and the Universe have changed in some way, making your prayer once again fresh and new.

Truthful, Present Tense & Positive

An effective Practical Prayer is always a statement of Truth. It's the Truth known to the one speaking the prayer: Truth known on a Universal level. Someone with no money who desires to live in an experience of prosperity can say, "I have plenty of money," but if he doesn't believe it's true, he will experience the result of his belief rather than the result of his words.

It is done as you believe, always. The statements of Truth that could be used to change those beliefs and achieve an experience of prosperity might be, "The Universe is Infinitely abundant, with resources beyond my comprehension. I am One with this Universe and have access to all of the richness and abundance that exists everywhere. I now live in the experience of this rich prosperity". As long as the words ring true for you, they'll work to activate your beliefs and bring about a change in your experience.

Practical Prayer is always spoken in the present tense – the time is now. Our desire is to change the immediate experience of our lives. There is no need to wait. If we accept a delay in our experience changing, we are showing a belief that we don't think we can experience it now. The Universe has been around for a long time and has far greater patience than we do! There might be times we feel a conflict making a statement of truth in the present tense, such as a person in the midst of an illness. If it's difficult to claim perfect health in the middle of the experience, simply adjust the statement until it is both immediate and resonates as Truth, i.e. "I know that my body is right now in the process of returning to perfect health and comfort".

The Universe always says "yes". Whatever idea is impressed upon it, the Law always responds in the affirmative. We speak our Word of Truth in the positive as well, ensuring that there is congruence between our intention and the results we will experience. If we pray for something not to happen, we are putting our attention and intention into what we don't want. The Law responds to what we're focused on. A student who affirms, "I don't want to get an F." is likely to get a different result than the one who claims, "I get an A".

Personal & Life-affirming

We always pray for ourselves. The goal is to create a new belief in our own mind, and thereby create a change in our life. Our individual, local mind is part of one infinite Mind, which creates everything. Practical Prayer is the method we use to introduce a new idea into the Infinite Mind, causing It to create a different condition or experience of life. When we want to help another person, we still pray for ourselves. In this case it's to create a new belief in our mind about what's possible for them. We are still connecting with the one Infinite Mind, rather than the individual, local mind of the other person.

When praying for another person it is important that they specifically request your support in prayer. We cannot choose what's someone else should desire, regardless of how obvious it might be to us. A dad desperately praying that his son get a great position on the football team will not help a boy who has a passion for ballet dancing. With their agreement, we can pray in full support. In any situation where a specific request has not been conveyed, you can always pray for the Highest and Best to unfold with Love and Ease for all involved. The prayer on page 47 is an example.

Effective prayer is life affirming, intended to bring an experience of more love and goodness and wholeness into the lives of the ones being prayed for. This isn't because destructive or limiting prayers won't work; it's because they tend to bring more limitation or destruction into the experience of the one praying and to all involved. In other words, they backfire. Praying for an adversary to get sick is one of the most effective ways for someone to bring illness into his or her own life.

The Steps to Practical Prayer

Each Practical Prayer follows a specific formula. The formula was distilled from the effective prayers done in all major religions and professional healers have proven it effective over the course of many decades. See Appendix A for a detailed explanation of the steps, or enroll in a foundational class in New Thought spiritual practices at a local organization or online for in-depth study. You can find listing and links at www.be-the-light.com.

RUR_2GR - Are You Ready to Get Results?

This simple mnemonic is your key to the steps of Practical Prayer. It's also a reminder that your Belief System (your personal BS) is the key to creating the life you desire. When you answer "Yes"

Using This Book

to the question "are you ready to get results?" a universe of possibilities opens to you.

In this book, icons are used to indicate each step. It's not necessary to know which words are part of which steps to make the prayer effective. They are shown as a learning aid to assist you in creating practical prayers of your own.

R Recognition (God Is)

U Unification (I Am)

R Realization/ Affirmation (I Know)

1 of 2: Refutation (It's Not)

2 of 2: Re-affirmation (Now I Really Know)

G Gratitude (I am Grateful)

R Release (I let it go)

"Yeah-buts"

The steps of Refutation and Re-affirmation are not included in all Practical Prayers. The objective of the prayer is to create a new belief in the one doing the prayer, and these steps serve the purpose of helping to resolve doubt. When our desires clash with our beliefs, we experience doubt.

As an example, when someone who wants to have more prosperity in her life states, "I have plenty of money" she might hear a little voice chime in saying, "yeah, but the checking account is overdrawn." Those "Yeah, buts" are an indicator of personal disbelief. When a "yeah-but" comes up, we include the two additional steps to refute the false belief and re-affirm the Truth that we want to embody. The refutation might be "any idea that there is not enough money in the Universe, or that I am undeserving of living a prosperous life is completely untrue. I now return this false idea to the place of powerlessness from which it came".

That would be followed by a repeat of the affirmation, "I have plenty of money." If the "yeah-but" chimes in again, use it as an indicator that there's more to that belief. Repeat the Refutation step, and once again re-affirm the Truth. Repeat the cycle until the yeah-but subsides. Always follow a Refutation with a repeat of your affirmation – end on an up note. Lather, rinse, repeat.

In a case where the yeah-but is persistent, you can take the guidance that you're attempting a larger step than you're ready for. You could refine the affirmation to something that's believable, or work with a healing prayer Practitioner or spiritual counselor to help uncover and change your hidden belief.

Using the Prayers

The longest distance in the world is the eighteen inches between the head and the heart. This book is about changing your beliefs, which live deep within and are brought into awareness through mental or intellectual processes. Reading the prayers in this book is good. Saying the words out loud is even better. To get really powerful results, you'll embody these new ideas as they settle into your head, your heart, and your gut.

When you choose one of the prayers to work with, get a very clear idea of what it is, specifically, that you wish to experience. It might be expressed clearly and completely as the prayer is written, or might benefit from a bit of personalization. There's a blank line right after the ❗ affirmation step where you can write in your own specific desire. Please remember to make it a positive, life-affirming, and believable statement of Truth in the present tense.

Done As You Believe

You'll know that your Practical Prayer work is effective by the changes you experience in your life. They might be immediate and obvious, or might be more gradual or subtle. Your life is a topographical map of your beliefs. That makes it pretty easy to discern the current state of your belief system – just look at your life. If you find yourself in a situation where the change you're seeking isn't coming about, it's time to dig into the beliefs you hold most deeply. You can do a Practical Prayer for clarity and insight. You can enlist the help of a spiritual counselor or healing prayer Practitioner, or quiet your mind in a meditative state and allow those hidden beliefs to be revealed.

Keep It Simple

The prayers in this book are short and succinct. This is intentional, so that in reading them you get an understanding of the content and flow. When creating your own prayers or adapting these, add as much to them as you'd like. Some prayers can last twenty minutes. They're not inherently better or more powerful because of their duration. The key is always for you to arrive in a place where you believe that the words you're using are true – or at least that they could be – and that your desired outcome is at hand.

You Are Perfect, Now

Our culture has ideas of right and wrong, of good and bad, and other judgments. There are shared ideas of beauty, of prosperity, of ethics and values, and so forth. These are all real and they are quite superficial. The Truth we are uncovering is the realization that everything is part of a single creation. Everything is God. Everything is Love. And everything is perfect, just as it is.

The changes we are creating through this prayer work are not to take something "bad" and make it "good"; our work, instead, is to accept the good that is already at hand, accept that it is already part of the Infinite One, and to create a new experience which fits more harmoniously with our desires. Some people like chocolate and others like vanilla. This process is about putting each together with their favored flavor.

Practical Prayers

"Some prayers are more effective than others. Some only help us to endure, while others transcend conditions, and demonstrate an invisible law which has power over the visible. In so far as our prayer is affirmative, it is creative of the desired result."

- Ernest Holmes, The Science of Mind

"Your word is the power you have to create. Your word is the gift that comes directly from God."

- don Miguel Ruiz, The Four Agreements

"To believe in the things you can see and touch is no belief at all, but to believe in the unseen is a triumph and a blessing."

- Abraham Lincoln

Perfect health & comfort

✴ There is One Power, one Infinite Intelligence, one Creator that has made everything that exists in the physical universe, and It continues to create. Every aspect of this Creation exists in perfect harmony within itself and in relation to all else. Everything I see, touch, or know is a creation of this One.

🧍 "Everything," of course, includes me. I, too, am the Creative Expression of the One. Every aspect of my life began as an idea in the mind of this Infinite Intelligence, and it all fits together in the perfect harmony of a single Creation.

❗ My body is this harmony. Every cell, every tissue, every organ, and enzyme is part of this one Perfect Creation, and it all works together in divine harmony. I am perfect health and perfect comfort. I live in divine balance and harmony.

---

insert your specific desire here

❓ Anything that causes me physical discomfort, distress, or disease is a temporary experience only and has nothing to do with the Truth of me. It is not a problem to be fixed, but simply an indication that I have the opportunity to come more fully into the balance, harmony, and experience of health that are my birthright.

‼ I claim my perfect health and harmony now. I know that anything that has been out of balance or physically challenging resolves immediately.

🧘 I am grateful for this perfect health, for my ability to state this Truth and know that it creates my experience.

🙏 With deep gratitude, I accept this good and know that it is so. *And so it is!*

Prayers for Physical Wellness

Perfect weight

There is only God, the One Infinite Creator, which has brought everything into form. No matter where I look, all I see is the Loving creation of this One. All distinct and different, and all good in its own special and specific way.

When I look in the mirror, I also see the Loving Creation of this One. I am God's Love taking form in this body – this living, moving, changing, adaptable, and perfectly designed body.

I know that my body is continuously changing, renewing, growing, and developing. So now, by action of this prayer, I choose to more fully experience the harmony, balance, and physical perfection that are my birthright. I claim my perfect weight (of _____) and my perfect size and shape (which I describe as _____), and I know that everything in my experience moves and shifts to support this new, grander expression of God's perfection as my body.

---

insert your specific desire here

Nothing stands in the way of this transformation. I let go of any mental blockage or obstruction, allowing it to resolve and dissolve into the nothingness from which it came.

These joyous, healthy and happy changes to my body happen immediately and continue to unfold in a way that fully supports my perfect health, vitality and comfort.

I am grateful for this delightful shift, for the healing which is the revealing of the true "me."

This Truth is spoken, and it is done.
And so it is!

Harmony and balance

There is only One. One Power, one Mind, one Intelligence that created everything in the world around me. It began with nothing – in darkness and void – and brilliantly brought forth all of the rich range of forms and forces that I experience. Because everything came from the One, all must by its nature fit perfectly in its place within the Whole. This is the Divine Harmony and balance of all of Creation.

I am part of this Creation, so I too must fit into it in perfect balance and harmony.

Every cell in my body is in harmony, within itself, with all of the surrounding cells and tissues and fluids and organs of my body, and with everything in my environment. This harmony and balance is the perfect health, which is my birthright, the Natural Order intended for my experience.

---

insert your specific desire here

Anything that appears to obstruct or interfere with this perfect health and harmony is a temporary distraction and is *not* the Truth.

I allow my mind and body to return easily and immediately to harmony, health, and comfort.

I am thankful for the Divine Goodness, grateful to live each moment in balance and harmony.

It is with gratitude for this goodness that I speak this Word of Truth, knowing that it is made manifest without hesitation. *And so it is!*

Prayers for Physical Wellness

Safe travel

Everything around me is part of One coherent Universe. All of the different things that seem separate and disconnected are, in fact, all part of this One. Just as each petal on a flower is part of the same plant, along with the stems and leaves and roots and thorns, all is One.

I am part of this one divine Creation. I, too, am connected with and growing as an idea in the one Mind. Everything that takes place in my life begins as a creative idea in the one Mind, and all of it fits together perfectly – a single Creation with billions of moving parts.

As I travel and move about, I encounter new and different places, activities, and experiences, yet I know they are all part of the One. In each moment, I am in my perfect place, having my perfect experience. I travel in safety and comfort, easily connecting with the joy and delight of each place and time.

---
insert your specific desire here

There are no problems, difficulties, or delays necessary.

All of my travels and activities fit together in joy, harmony, and peace. I know that I am in my perfect place, experiencing my Divine Good in each moment.

I am grateful for my safe and happy travels, knowing that all is moving and unfolding in perfect order.

Knowing this is true, I speak it to the Law, which always says "Yes"!
And so it is!

Successful surgical procedure

Everything is in its perfect place. Every person is on his or her perfect path. All of Creation fits together in the richness and harmony of a finely woven tapestry. There is nothing that is not part of the One grand design. Everything is an aspect of this One – a thread woven into the Infinite tapestry of the Universe.

I am this One. Every person involved in this surgical procedure is this One taking individual form. The surgeon, the patient, and the anesthesiologist are this One. The nurses, the technicians, and the support staff are this One. The caring friends and family members are all this One.

Every step of this procedure is the One weaving itself into a new pattern. It is the opportunity for the surgeons to share their skill. It is an avenue through which the patient's body can come into a new, more healthful, and more comfortable form. It is a space in which each one involved can witness and experience Love showing up in a new way.

---

insert your specific desire here

There is no need for problems or complications or "bad news" in any form. Any worry or concern about a difficulty is easily resolved into the insight that the "good" outcome I desire is equally possible, so I focus my attention on that.

The desired outcome is at hand. As good as I can imagine and even better.

I am grateful to know that this success is in process and give thanks for my opportunity to share my love and direct my energy and intention toward this perfect result.

I let this strong belief loose into the Law, knowing that the Law is already saying "Yes!"

And so it is!

Prayers for Physical Wellness

Health, vitality, and wholeness

There is only One Power, One Mind, One Source. This One has created everything, and because its creation is all One, I know that every part of Creation fits together perfectly with every other part in perfect balance and harmony.

I am part of this Creation, so I, too, am perfect balance and harmony.

I experience this in my body as health, vitality, and wholeness. I am perfect health and comfort, right now and always. This harmony and balance is my birthright.

---

insert your specific desire here

Any discomfort, distress, or disease is a temporary interruption of my standard experience of health and wholeness. There is no truth or power to it, so I turn my attention away from symptoms or conditions to the Truth behind them.

I am perfect health, harmony, and balance. My body returns to its intended perfection immediately.

I give thanks for this Healing, which is simply the revealing of the Truth.

I let it be.
And so it is!

Love throughout my life

✴ God is Love, and God is all there is.

☥ Therefore I, too, am Love.

❗ So I experience love in every part of my life. There is only Love and I am it. I am…

---
insert your specific desire here

🧘 Whenever I feel an absence of love or lack of love, I know that I am being invited to open myself more fully to the love that surrounds me.

‼️ I am God's Infinite Love. I accept that love, now and always.

🧘 I am grateful for the love that I am, that I have, and that I share.

🙏 I let this be so.
And so it is!

Prayers for Emotional Wholeness

Perfect relationships

※ There is only Love. The Universe was created as an act of Love, and everything in it is made of that Infinite Love.

🕯 I, too, am a creation of this Infinite Love, and everything in my life is a new and different appearance of this One Love.

! I have my perfect relationships. I am drawn to the perfect people and they are drawn to me. I relax into the awareness that we are all divine and wonderful expressions of the One Loving Spirit and the way we fit together is Love itself. I know by action of this prayer that this Love is now blossoming in joy and harmony and fun for me and all involved.

---
insert your specific desire here

? Anything that appears to stand in the way of this divine goodness is merely a shadow created by circumstance. It has no power or substance and dissolves instantly in the awareness of the presence of God's love.

‼ I experience loving, joyous, harmonious relationships. I feel the love. I am the Love.

🙏 I am grateful for it.

🧍 I know this is the Truth and I release it into the Law, knowing that it is already changing my life.
And so it is!

My life fills with Love

- There is only Love. Everything that exists is that Infinite Love in a unique form.

- I, too, am that Love, and everything I experience is yet another aspect of that same Limitless Love.

- My life is filled with Love. Every encounter, every conversation, every relationship is that Divine Love taking form. I know that I attract love and that I *am* love. I have perfect loving relationships.

---

insert your specific desire here

- I relax into this Love and accept it with a grateful heart.

- Knowing that this is the Truth, I release it into the Law. *And so it is!*

Prayers for Emotional Wholeness

I live in peace and harmony

Everything comes from One divine Source. The Infinite Mind of God creates everything that makes up the universe and everyone in it.

This Creation includes me, (and _____), and everyone I encounter. Every relationship and every exchange is, in fact, God interacting with God.

Knowing this, I immediately understand that every relationship is yet another expression of the Infinite, moving against itself to bring a new demonstration of that Love into being. Every relationship is the divine harmony of One Power.

There are many musical notes and tones, each wonderful in its own way. Combining them brings about harmony.

When the combination of notes is discordant, it is immediately obvious, and the musicians are able to adjust their interaction to a more pleasant resonance. When something other than harmony and peace arise in my relationships, it is an indication that something can be adjusted. No one is wrong or bad – it is simply an opportunity to shift to a more peaceful, loving, and harmonious note.

I adjust easily and gently, as does everyone with whom I interact. My relationships are always this supreme harmony, bringing peace and joy and love to all involved.

---

insert your specific desire here

I am grateful for my awareness of the harmony and the dissonance, and for the loving and gentle way that the Universe responds and adjusts to bring that harmony into my life.

I let this be so
And so it is!

Surrounded in Love

✳ There is only Love. Everything that exists is the One Infinite Mind sharing its own substance as all it creates. This creative sharing of Self can only be an expression of Love, so I know that everything is Love.

👼 This includes me. I am a unique and wonderful example of this Infinite Love, and everything in my life is more of this Love.

❗ I turn my attention from the distractions around me to the Truth behind them. I am surrounded by Love. I am loved and loving, and I attract ever more love and joy in every moment. I have my perfect loving relationships.

---
insert your specific desire here

🧘 I am grateful to be this Love and to share this Love.

🧍 I release this intention, stake my claim, and let the Love flow in my life.
And so it is!

Prayers for Emotional Wholeness

I breathe God's Love

God is Love. God is the Light. God is divine Creative goodness sharing itself through its Creation.

I am the light. I am Love made manifest.

Everyone I encounter sees me as Love. I see everyone I encounter as Love. God breathes me in every moment, and I am the joy, the peace, the harmony, the success, the joyous creation and creativity of the One. I smile. I laugh. I breathe. And I allow my divine God-essence to unfold as Love through every experience.

---

insert your specific desire here

There is no struggle or strain. I have no fear and simply allow any concerns to be revealed, addressed, and resolved.

I breathe God's Love in all that I do and all that I am.

I gratefully shine God's Light of Love.

I am Love.
And so it is!

Loving and intimate sex

Love is all there is. Everything, everyone, everywhere is a demonstration of this Infinite Love in its own unique and special way. And all of it fits together in perfect love, harmony, and joy.

I, too, am an expression of this Love. I am this Infinite Love made real, right here and right now. I am a being of Love, living in a world of love.

Therefore I know that I attract and embody love in all ways. I am a physical, sensual, sexual being, and I attract and embody my perfect sexual experiences. My sex partner and activities are the expression of Infinite Love as physical sharing and pleasure. Our intimate connection is Love made manifest.

---
insert your specific desire here

There is nothing improper or inappropriate or dirty. There is no cause for shame, struggle, or despair.

There is only Love, pouring into my physical world as a joyous, passionate, tender, loving, exciting, orgasmic, fun-filled, and completely appropriate sex life.

I am grateful for this physical expression of love, thankful for my perfect partner and this wonderful way that my experience of connectedness takes form.

With gratitude, I accept this perfect sexual expression of my true, loving self and know that it is so.
And so it is!

Prayers for Emotional Wholeness

I choose loving relationships

There is only Love. The entire universe is a creation of Love; one creative God-power sharing itself as its creation. That creativity, that sharing of self, is an expression of pure Love.

Everything in the Universe is a creation of Love, including me. It includes each person I connect with. I am that Love, and as an expression of that Love, I attract more and more of that same Love into my life.

I choose Love. I choose to live in Love, to be Love, to be loving, and to be loved. The vibration of my conscious energy steps up to a higher level as I more become more fully aware of my connection to the Love that I am. I become an even greater expression of Love in every area of my life and attract even more love and more loving relationships.

---

insert your specific desire here

There is no power that blocks or obstructs this deepening, expanding expression of Love. Anything that appears to be standing between me and the full experience of these deep and loving relationships is an illusion – a shadow. As such, it vanishes immediately in the bright light of my new understanding

I am Love. I am loved. I have my perfect loving relationships, right now and always.

I share this Love and express this Love with deep gratitude. I accept this Love as the gift that it is.

I know, right now, without doubt or reservation that this perfect Love is my life now. This is the Truth of me.
And so it is!

Money to spend, share and save

- This is an abundant Universe. There are billions of stars in billions of galaxies. One glance at the night sky is ample proof that this is an infinitely abundant Universe. A forest has billions of leaves on thousands of trees, all living and growing in a connected ecosystem. The economy is another of God's Creations, with money as the currency that flows in exchange and balance. All of these uncountable riches are part of one divine Creative Expression – a dazzling work of art on God's canvas.

- I am part of this creation, another example of God's Love/Energy taking form. I am surrounded by and immersed in the limitless abundance of God's good. The good that exists throughout creation is available and accessible to me in the same unquestionable way that there is oxygen available and accessible in my next breath.

- Knowing this, I know that there is plenty of money available and accessible to me right now and always. I am in the flow of the economic system, sharing my gifts and accepting bountiful compensation. I have plenty of money for all of my activities and endeavors.

---
insert your specific desire here

- Any idea that there is not enough money is absurd. That's like saying that God could run out of star-stuff and not be able to create another star. The notion that there's plenty everywhere, except for me, is simply not true.

- I have plenty of money to spend, to share, and to save. Right now and always. I am a good steward of my resources and engage in activities that support my life of prosperity.

- I am grateful for the good in my life, for the cash in my pocket, and the balance in my bank accounts. I give thanks for the resources at hand that allow me to share my gifts and participate fully and joyously in life.

Knowing that I am a full participant in God's infinitely abundant Universe, I set this Word in motion, releasing it to the Law and knowing that Universe responds with a resounding "Yes"!
And so it is!

I live in prosperity, joy, and love

This is an abundant Universe, and everything in it is created by the One Infinite Spirit and shared in love.

I am also a creation of the One and I share in all of the Abundant Richness.

I have everything, right now, to live my life in prosperity, joy, and love.

---
insert your specific desire here

Any idea that there is not enough, that my life experience is in any way limited, is just plain wrong.

There is plenty. Everything that I require for a full and rich and prosperous life is at hand and is available to me at exactly the perfect moment.

I am grateful for this prosperity. I accept these gifts with delight.

I speak this Truth of my abundant life into the Law, knowing that the Law always responds immediately, continuously, and without hesitation.
And so it is!

Life is rich, joyous and full

✳︎ All comes from One Source. That Source is the Creator, the One we call God. This One began with itself and nothing else and It created everything in our world by sharing itself as its Creation. This Universe is Infinite, with uncountable billions of stars in the sky and billions of planets around the stars. Right here on planet Earth, there are uncountable billions of trees, drops of water, and grains of sand. This Universe is created in Limitless Abundance. Everything that exists is an individualized facet of this One Infinite Expression.

👤 The same must be true of me. I am a unique part of God's creation, carrying and sharing my own specific and wonderful gifts of God. As a Divinely Created member of the Infinite Family, I share in all the abundance of the Universe.

❗ I have everything I desire and require to live my life richly and joyously and fully. I share my gifts with love and I accept the prosperity this Infinite, Loving Universe shares with me.

---

insert your specific desire here

❓ Any idea that there is not enough, that I might be undeserving, or that there is need for struggle is simply wrong. The Creator that made billions of galaxies cannot run out of riches just when it gets to me.

‼️ I accept my prosperity, knowing that I am directly connected to the Infinite Creative Power of the Universe.

🙏 I accept with gratitude, giving thanks for all that I have, and for the Divine Creation that I am.

🧍 I release this Truth into the Law, knowing it is most certainly so.
And so it is!

Prayers for Financial Prosperity

A life of opulent comfort

There is One Power, One Infinite Source of All that Is. This One began with an idea, and with that idea created the Universe in all of its rich, limitless diversity and depth.

This same Power created me. It gave me, in its own image, the same ability to tap into the Infinite abundance of the Universe to create my own life.

I use this ability well. I am prosperous and joyously create my life, my work, my career, and my business in opulent comfort.

---

insert your specific desire here

There is nothing that stands in the way of this Infinite Power and nothing that stands in the way of my prosperity and success.

I am prosperous. I am successful, now and at all times. I relax into my wonderful experience of abundance, knowing that it is my birthright. I know that every step and task is done in peace, joy, and harmony.

I am grateful for these gifts and for my awareness of my inborn ability to create my life in such a rich and wonderful way.

Knowing that this is the Truth, I release it into the Law and let the Law respond.
And so it is!

Joyously doing my perfect work

✦ There is One Creative Power that created – and continues to create – everything that exists. Everything that I see, touch, taste, smell, or know is created by this One.

✦ I am part of this Creation, experiencing this life and this moment in a way that is uniquely "me." And the One Power continues to create through me.

! I share my skills, my gifts, and talents to bring this Creation into its next great expression. My presence, my work, and my creativity are bringing more love, more joy, more harmony, and more good to my life, to my world, and to those around me. This is my perfect work, which I do with joy.

---

insert your specific desire here

? It need never feel draining, limited, or overwhelming.

‼ My work is my opportunity to bring this Creative Power more fully into focus in my life and the world around me.

🙏 I am grateful for my gifts and my ability to share them.

🧍 I speak this Word as my truth, knowing I am joyously doing my perfect work.
And so it is!

Satisfaction and success

There is one Mind, one Power, one Infinite Intelligence that sets the pattern, which takes form in the world around me. Everything begins as an idea in this Mind.

Everything, including me and every experience I have. The mind I think with is this same Mind, and the process is exactly the same. So I set my intention with the clear understanding that what I create in my mind begins to happen immediately in my life.

I am successful and satisfied in all of my endeavors. All of my activities and interactions bring joy and goodness to me and all involved.

---

insert your specific desire here

Nothing can stand in the way of this goodness.

The Infinite moves forth into my experience through this divinely guided process.

I am thankful for my joy and success and for the Universal Law, which makes it happen.

This Word is spoken and it is Done.
And so it is!

Infinite mind creates through me

There is a single Mind, one Intelligence that brings everything into Creation. All is the expression, the out-picturing of this One. Everything that I see, or touch or taste or smell or hear began as an idea in this Infinite Mind.

I began as an idea in this Mind, and my mind creates in the same way.

I am part of the Infinite Creator and embody this creative power in a way that is uniquely and wonderfully "me."

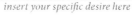
insert your specific desire here

There is nothing to block or obstruct this Creative action.

I know that my ideas, thoughts, and intentions always create that which is uplifting and life affirming for all involved. This is the Infinite creating through and as me.

I am grateful for this creative power, for the good works brought into being by my intention and action.

I accept it and allow it and let it be so.
And so it is!

My work is valuable and rewarding

In all the universe there is one Infinite Creative Power. This One shapes and forms its unlimited substance into the rich diversity of everything that exists. Particles, people, and planets are just a few of the ways that this substance takes form. And everything, in its own unique way, is a perfect Creation of the One.

I, too, am this Infinite Substance taking form. I am this limitless perfection showing up as me. My mind is part of the same Mind that creates everything, and I use this same intentional process to create the experiences of my life.

My work is an example of this creative process. I express my unique perspective and share my one-of-a-kind combination of talents, skills, and experience. My perfect work is a demonstration of love, supporting and benefiting me and everyone it touches.

---
insert your specific desire here

There are no unimportant jobs.

Everything that happens is another way that the one infinite Power shares itself. My work is valuable, rewarding, and greatly appreciated. I do it well, and I do it with joy, satisfaction, and great success.

I am grateful for my perfect work and the fun, harmonious, successful, and loving way that I do it.

This is my Truth. I speak it into the Law, knowing that the Law responds with an immediate Yes!
And so it is!

Successful completion

- Spirit is all there is. One infinite Mind, one creative Intelligence in back of everything and everyone at every moment. This One creates everything that is. The entire universe is a project created by the One.

- I am part of this project, a living, breathing, thinking product of this creative enterprise. I share in this ability to Create, using the same infinite Power and Intelligence channeled through me.

- My current project comes together in the same perfect way. All of the details are addressed. All of the elements fit together seamlessly. Each requirement is easily met or exceeded. Everyone involved is pleased, satisfied, and enthusiastic about this completely successful outcome.

---
insert your specific desire here

- Nothing stands in the way of this. Nothing.

- This project is an idea born in the Mind of God, taking form through the action and creativity of me and of everyone involved. Successful completion is at hand right now or on schedule with impeccable timing.

- I am deeply grateful for this successful outcome and for the joyous and effortless way it comes about.

- Knowing that success is already real in the Mind of God, I speak this Word acknowledging that it is the Truth, and let it take form.
  And so it is!

Prayers for Perfect Work & Creativity

A wonderful event[†]

※ Love is all there is. It takes on an infinite variety of forms and appearances, but at the heart of everything, there is Love. Since I know that all is Love and that all is One, I know that everything fits together by the very nature of its oneness.

※ I am this Love. My event, _____ is this Love. All of the elements and ingredients – the people, the materials, the program, the space, the weather, the food, the entertainment – all are this Love, too.

! Every aspect of this event comes together in exquisite perfection. It is the harmony and beauty of God's Love expressing itself as this wonderful event. This is the activity of God, bringing good and more good to me and to every person involved.

------

insert your specific desire here

? There is no problem, no difficulty, and certainly no disaster necessary. Anything less than the perfect unfolding of this event is unacceptable. It is a false idea and is returned immediately to the empty darkness from which it came.

!! This event is already perfect in the Mind of the One. I now affirm and allow it to fully take form as a joyous and wonderful experience for each one involved.

🙏 I am deeply grateful for this fabulous event, for my ability to know this Truth and speak this Word.

🕇 I release it to the Law
And so it is!

[†] Adjust the description and name of the event to describe your specific program. Add or alter the event details to encompass the accommodations, transportation, timing, and other elements that are key to the success of your event.

Harmony and peace

⁕ There is only Love. Everything is part of this One Love, showing up as something new and different and original, yet the Truth is that there is only the One.

This means that everything I am is this One Love. Everything I experience is also this One Love. I am fundamentally connected to everything through – and as – this Universe of Love.

I live in peace, relaxing into the knowledge that every aspect of this one-ness exists in perfect harmony with all the rest of Creation.

---
insert your specific desire here

Anything that appears or feels to me to be less than this perfect Peace, this infinite Love, this divine Harmony is a shadow that falsely blocks the Truth. I now allow it to disappear into the nothingness from which it came.

I turn my attention once more to the Love, the Harmony, and the Peace, which are the foundation of All. This is a deep and profound peace, and I open myself to it in this situation and at all times.

My life is blessed by this awareness, and I am deeply grateful to relax into this space of peace.

I release this now, knowing without doubt that it is the Truth. *And so it is!*

Prayers of Spirit

One with the Divine

There is One Power, One Infinite Intelligence that created all that is and continues to create it.

This includes me. It has to include me. I am created from that same Infinite Source, from the same substance of all Creation. So I am not just connected to this One – I am part of it. Everything I am is the creation of this Infinite Mind.

By action of this prayer I choose to be aware in every moment of my connection to the One. I am a unique and beautiful flower planted firmly in this rich, Divine Soil. I know that…

---
insert your specific desire here

Any idea that I am separate from the One Source is a mirage.

It dissolves immediately with my awareness of the Truth, that I am one with the One.

I am thankful for this awareness, now and always.

I speak this intention for my continuous awareness of the Truth, knowing that I am connected to the One.
And so it is!

Connection to God

✳ There is only God. In the beginning, before there was anything, there was God. With Infinite Power and Creative inspiration, God shared Its Energy and Substance and brought all that we experience into being.

👼 Everything in the Universe is the Creation of God. Everything that exists is this Divine expression of God's good. As a participant in this universe, I too must be the divine expression of God's good.

❗ I feel it. I connect with my True nature as a living, breathing, thinking, feeling part of God. I am aware that God is all around me and that God is within me. Turning inward, I easily experience my connection with the Infinite. I relax into the awareness that I am One with God.

---
insert your specific desire here

🧘 I am grateful to know this. I am grateful to feel this. Most importantly, I am grateful to be this loving, intelligent, and balanced participant in God's creation.

🧍 Knowing that this is True, and knowing that my awareness of my connection with God deepens and strengthens every time the thought crosses my mind, I release this Creative Word to the Law, and know that it is so.
And so it is!

The next step is revealed

There is One Mind, One Infinite Intelligence that has created the Universe and everything in it. That Creation began as a clear, definite idea in the One Mind with all of the rich detail unfolding as the Idea took form.

My mind is the same Mind taking individual form. My mind creates in the same way and has access to everything available to the One Mind.

I think with the same clarity. My next perfect idea, my next step, my next opportunity to express my true Greatness is revealed to me clearly, gently, and immediately.

insert your specific desire here

There is no need for confusion, distraction, or delay. I relax and release any thoughts, memories, or fears that have filled my consciousness.

I now allow that next great insight or idea to reveal itself in joy and peace.

I am grateful for this clarity and for my ability to create my life according to my desires.

Accepting this Divine gift, I speak this Truth into the Law and let it be so.
And so it is!

Centered in the Love of God

There is one Power, one creative Force in back of everything. This One started with an idea in Mind, an intention for creation. It put that idea into effect through the Laws of nature. Everything that I experience in the world around me is a result – an effect – of this Divine creative First Cause.

I am surrounded by God's Creation. Its rich beauty and powerful presence extends to infinity in every direction around me. From this perspective, I can know with certainty that I am centered in the Love of God.

With this awareness, I relax. I let loose any tight control I've taken to maneuver my life into the form I desire. I allow God to create my next joyous new experience.

---

insert your specific desire here

Any notion that I am on my own to create the life I desire, or that I have to figure everything out, is simply not true.

God has been doing it all along, so right now, by action of this prayer, I consciously and specifically turn it over to the Infinite. I know that I am centered in the Infinite Love of God, right now, in every moment and in every way. I accept all of these blessings. I reflect God's Love in all that I do, in every thought, with every breath. I attract good and more good into my life.

I am grateful for this new and deeper awareness of my connection with the Creator, thankful to feel this immense creative power within me.

With deep gratitude for all of the good that surrounds me, enfolds me, and flows through my life, I set this intention to live in the awareness that I am centered in the Love of the Infinite, and let it be.
And so it is!

Aware of My Spiritual Nature

There is one Power, which I call God, that creates everything. In the beginning there was only God. God shared itself in creating the Universe I now experience. Everything in the universe is part of this divine Creative Expression. It all came from the One, so there cannot be anything else.

I, too, must be part of the creative expression of the One. I, too, am created by God. All that I am, all that I ever was, and all that I ever will be is God's creative Intention taking form as me.

Knowing this, I know that all I am and all I do takes place within the loving embrace of God. When I feel joyous, I am expressing God's infinite potential. When I feel longing or desire, I am a channel for God's urge to create something new. Through all of it, I am totally aware of my spiritual nature.

---
insert your specific desire here

I have no need for anguish or despair. These guiding signals appear as gentle contrasts, allowing me to settle more comfortably into my awareness of God's Love.

The Hand of God is my hand. The Path of God is marked by my footsteps. The Love of God is present in me at every moment, in every action.

I am in deep gratitude for this awareness and relax easily into the spiritual strength of God.

I speak this Word, aware that it carries the creative authority of God's own Word and know that it is so.
And so it is!

Peace of mind

✳ There is One Creative Power, one Divine loving presence in back of everything. Each decision and event is part of the One expression of Love, and everything fits perfectly into its place in Creation. There is only the One, sharing and showing itself in richly diverse forms. Because it is all One, I can know without a doubt that every aspect of Creation fits perfectly into the Whole.

🧍 I am part of Creation, for there is nothing else I could be. My existence is proof that I, too, am part of the Infinite Love of the Creator. Therefore, I know that everything in my life experience fits perfectly together with every other aspect of my life and into its perfect place in creation.

! This harmony, this perfect balance is the natural order of the Universe. I relax into the certain knowledge that everything is in its perfect place, unfolding in its perfect way. My mind is at peace, knowing that all is in Divine Order.

---
insert your specific desire here

? I release any fear or judgment, any concern that there is a problem needing to be fixed.

‼ I turn it over to the Creator, knowing that the balance and perfection in the situation are becoming clear to me. I am at peace.

🙏 With gratitude for this insight into the Wisdom and the Power of the One…

🧍 I speak this Truth and release it to the Law, knowing it is so. *And so it is!*

Prayers of Spirit

Clarity

✴ I know that there is only one Mind: one Infinite Intelligence, one creative Source of everything, every moment, and every idea. There is only one Mind; that Mind is perfect.

🕺 That Mind is my mind. As a full-time participant in this Universe that's been created, I know that my mind is part of the one infinite Mind.

❗ Anything that is known anywhere can be available and accessible everywhere. Therefore I know, by the creative power of my Word and the action of this prayer, that everything required for a deep and full understanding of the current situation is made known to me, gently, easily, and immediately. I am clearly guided in my next perfect steps. All of this unfolds with delightfully perfect timing.

---
insert your specific desire here

❓ There is no confusion, distraction, or befuddlement in the Mind of the Creator. That Mind is perfect.

‼ That Mind is my mind, now. Any false beliefs that might be hidden in my consciousness are made known to me and resolve into clear awareness and perfect guidance.

🙇 I am grateful for this clarity and give thanks for the wisdom, insight, and guidance that are now at hand.

🧍 I accept it. I step into it. I embody it, and I let it be so.
And so it is!

Divine Order

✳ A single Creative Power is in back of everything I see, everything I touch, and everything I understand. This One has been the power of all Creation since the beginning of time and continues to Create. An idea, formed in this creative Mind, sets the Law in motion and causes that idea to take form in the outer world of experience.

👼 That Mind is my mind, too. My thoughts have the same creative power. The Law responds to my words in the same way to bring those ideas into form.

❗ Because I am part of the One, I know that my creative thoughts fit perfectly into the One grand Creation. Everything in my life is unfolding in Divine Order. I feel completely at peace.

---
insert your specific desire here

❓ There is no imbalance or discord. Anything that seems uncomfortable or undesirable is simply the outward appearance of a new thought or new idea fitting into the experience of my life.

‼️ All is in its perfect place. Every facet of my life is in divine Right Order.

🙇 With a deep feeling of thanks, I accept this Truth.

🧍 I release this creative Word into the Law. It responds as it always does, fulfilling the Word as spoken.
And so it is!

Highest & best with Love & ease

There is only Love. Everything, everyone, everywhere is an idea born in the creative mind of God now taking form in space and time. This sharing of creative energy is an act of pure Love, so I know there is only Love.

I am that Infinite Love taking form in a way that is uniquely me. Every person, each creature, and all activity is this Infinite Love taking definite form. There is only Love.

I know and affirm that…

---
the good that I'm claiming

is now unfolding as the highest and best experience, with love and ease for me and each one involved.

There is no power or force that stands in opposition to this Good. Any fear, doubt, or idea of hesitation dissipates immediately and permanently into the nothingness from which it came.

There is only Love. It is now appearing in my life as the highest and best, with love and ease for all of us.

I am grateful for it… thankful for the Good that is now at hand. I am in gratitude for the Law that allows me to create this wonderful new experience and for the joyous way that it honors and elevates everyone involved.

I release this Word of Truth into the Infinite Mind of God, knowing this good is already under way.
And so it is!

Perfect weather

✴ Everything fits together in Divine Perfection. All of Creation is connected – by the obvious interactions I observe every day and the subtle interweaving of all matter, energy, and life everywhere. That connectedness takes form as weather – sunshine and clouds, high-pressure and low, that all come together in grand patterns that cover the planet. All of it fits together in perfection, the creation of the same Intelligent Power that creates everything.

👤 I am part of this grand pattern. I am in my perfect place, having my perfect experience. At this occasion, it fits together in Divine Harmony.

❗ The sunshine and clouds, the rain and snow, the warm and cool are all part of the One Creation, and I know and affirm that everything is coming together for a perfect weather experience.

---
insert your specific desire here

❓ The weather is not a problem. I let go of any judgment or critique of how it "should be". I simply allow Divine Order to reveal itself.

‼ The weather is perfect for this occasion, for me and all involved.

🙏 I am deeply grateful for the wonderful way that this all comes together. In gratitude I speak this Word.

🕴 I release it to the Law, knowing that the Law responds as it always does with a loud resounding "Yes!"
And so it is!

Prayers of Spirit

Mealtime Prayer

※ I am grateful for the abundant Good that surrounds and supplies me and each one here. We live in an Infinite Universe filled with limitless richness. It's one Creation with immeasurable depth and variety.

This abundance that surrounds us is also within us. I am part of this unlimited Good and so is each one present.

! This bread that we break, this meal that we share, is the One sharing itself, supplying itself, and supporting itself. I bless this meal and each one here. This is both nourishment for the body and an opportunity for us to share awareness of the richness that is present for us in all ways.

---
insert your specific desire here

I am grateful for this meal and this time of sharing. I give thanks for the food and the preparers and each one involved in bringing it together for this blessed moment. I am thankful for each one here.

This time is blessed, and each one here is fed and filled and nourished in exactly the perfect way.
And so it is!

Peace throughout the world

🔆 Everything is connected. There is one Power and Presence that shares itself in many forms. The forms may appear to be separate, but in back of the appearance there is the One. All of Creation is this One showing itself in a unique way.

👼 I am this infinite One taking personal form. Each individual is this One, all with our own perspective, our own desires, our own path, and our own story. Each is distinct, each is unique, and still each is part of the One.

❗ Knowing this, I know that everything, everyone everywhere, fits together into one cohesive Whole. We are all One. We are each part of the One. The parts all fit together in the perfect harmony that is peace itself. I claim this experience of peace and harmony, right now and continually for myself and for those around me.

---

insert your specific desire here

❓ In any situation where the parts of the Whole do not appear to be fitting in perfect harmony, I choose to know better. The idea that conflict or hostility or hatred is necessary or part of the natural order is simply untrue. I allow these wrong ideas to dissolve back into the empty shadows from which they came.

‼️ Peace and harmony are the natural order. All is part of the One, so I now know and affirm that anything that seems to show separateness, discord, or aggression easily and immediately resolves into the perfect harmony that is peace itself.

🧍 I am grateful for this good, proud to be the Ambassador of Peace. I am grateful to bear witness to this newfound harmony and give thanks for the wonderful way this peace now appears in the world around me.

I know this good is at hand, this Peace, which surpasses all human understanding, is here now. I speak this Word of Truth. I release it to the Creative Law of the universe and know with certainty that it is so.
And so it is!

Two Prayers for a Perfect Group Meeting

The prayers of invocation on the next two pages use very similar content; invoking an experience of the highest and best to unfold with love and ease for all involved. The "God" version uses spiritual language and specifically refers to God. The "stealth" version sets the same powerful intention using everyday secular language.

You could use the "stealth" version to open a business meeting or project, or in some other context where the God-oriented terminology might feel awkward or uncomfortable. I've described the activity as a project, but you can easily substitute "meeting," "event," or whatever word most accurately describes what you're involved in.

Use the difference between the two prayers to help you understand your own beliefs about how and where you're comfortable expressing your spiritual nature in front of others.

Perfect Group Meeting
- a "God" prayer Invocation

There is one Mind, one infinite Love/Intelligence, which I call God. This One shares itself through and as everything that It creates. Each person, every idea, and all activities are part of this One. There is nothing outside of this One, so I know that God is right here, right now.

I am this infinite Love/Intelligence taking form and so is each person here. Every idea is born in the Mind of the One. Every word is God's infinite Intelligence. Every interaction brings about a deeper understanding of this limitless wisdom.

This meeting is an infinite Idea taking particular form. This is the Divine Mind of God sharing itself through many channels, allowing good and more good to come into the lives of each one present and each one we touch. The insights are profound. The guidance is clear. The gifts that each one brings are joyously recognized and deeply appreciated. This time together unfolds in perfection.

---
insert your specific desire here

We easily move past any idea of separation or that we're limited or constrained by something that has happened before.

Any individual requirements or specific agendas are easily incorporated. We are working together and bring out the best ideas for what is possible.

I am grateful for this good and for the wonderful way that this meeting progresses. I give thanks for the unique combination of Love and Wisdom that each one brings to the group.

Feeling this gratitude, I know this time together is blessed. This meeting is a sacred activity and a tremendous success. *And so it is!*

Perfect Group Meeting

- a "stealth" prayer for an exercise in excellence

✳ We are together here now for something wonderful. This is an Exercise in Excellence.

🧍 Each of us has skills and strengths and knowledge. As we meet today, we're each bringing all of these gifts to this project (or _____) that we have in common.

! All of our diverse ideas and individual perspectives are already blending together. They continue to combine in ways that bring about great new ideas that go beyond what any of us can do on our own. Each voice is heard. Every good idea is welcome. We let the inspiration flow, and our success is greater than any of us have yet imagined.

_____
insert your specific desire here

? We easily move past any idea that we're limited or constrained by what's happened before.

‼ Any individual requirements or specific agendas are easily incorporated. We are all working together and bring out the best ideas for what is possible in this project (or _____).

🙏 I thank each one involved for his or her participation. I am grateful for the willingness to step up with enthusiasm to create something great.

🕴 As this exercise in excellence begins, I already know it's a tremendous success!
And so it is!

The Lord's Prayer

The Lords Prayer is one of the most widely repeated prayers in the world. It comes from the Sermon on the Mount in the book of Matthew: Chapter 6, verses 9-13. It's shown below, with the seven steps of Practical Prayer noted.

- Our Father which art in Heaven, Hallowed be thy name.
- Thy kingdom come. Thy will be done in earth, as it is in Heaven.
- Give us this day our daily bread. And forgive us our debts, as we forgive our debtors.
- And lead us not into temptation,
- but deliver us from evil (or error):
- For thine is the kingdom, and the power, and the glory,
- for ever.
  And so it is!

Pray like Jesus

In the passage immediately before this powerful prayer, Jesus gave a detailed explanation that this is a model for how to pray. He even urged his throng of listeners to avoid repeating any one prayer by rote – even this one. His guidance instead was to become quiet, go within (he used the metaphor of a closet), and pray in a way that will create results.

(Matt 6:6-9 King James version) But thou, when thou pray, enter into thy closet, and when thou hast shut thy door, pray to thy Father which is in secret; and thy Father which see in secret shall reward thee openly.

But when ye pray, use not vain repetitions, as the heathen do: for they think that they shall be heard for their much speaking.

Be not ye therefore like unto them: for your Father knoweth what things ye have need of, before ye ask him.

After this manner therefore pray ye: Our Father which art in heaven, Hallowed be thy name...

> Prayer is a yearning
> of the heart.

Authority & Accountability

It's Not My Fault!

Practical Prayer and the New Thought tradition of spirituality are based on the understanding that each one of us creates our own life experience through the beliefs we hold. We understand that it's done unto you as you believe. Some people take this to mean that whatever is wrong with their life is their fault. They want to know if the philosophy claims that they're somehow to blame for their unfortunate state of affairs. The answer is no. And yes.

Let's examine this idea in pieces, starting at the end, with someone's unfortunate state of affairs. New Thought is anchored on the belief that we live in a Universe of Oneness, where everything is good and everything is God. In our experience we sense contrasts: darkness when the light is hidden, cold when the heat is elsewhere, fear when the love is not obvious.

When we label something as "good" or "bad," we're making a judgment. In fact, experiences might just as easily be sorted into categories of "pleasant/unpleasant" or "joyful/educational" instead of "good/bad". There are many stories about people having undesirable experiences or seeing that things could be better which have inspired them to go out and change the world. Every creation and invention throughout history has been an example of someone seeing how the current state of affairs could be improved.

In order to find fault or assign blame, we label the experience as bad and then point a finger. If the experience were good, we'd use the word "credit" to attach a value judgment and then let it bolster our ego. Blame is a concept of how people think others are judging them. It is completely dis-empowering in that it labels the experience and then turns control of the emotion over to others. Saying something is our fault – or not – combines the negative judgment of the experience with an idea that we are somehow victims of circumstance.

We prefer the notions of authority and accountability. Authorship is the power each of us has to create our life. Accountability means that we get to live with whatever it is we've created. The good news is that it's a repeating cycle. We are free at any time to look at the life we've created and choose something different.

So, is it your fault that you're life is going the way it is? Let's hope so, because that means you have the ability to choose, and the same power you used to make your experience unpleasant can be used to turn it around.

Praying for Others

People often ask if Practical Prayer can be used to influence or affect someone else's life. The answer is Yes! When you think about it, you'll realize that the answer must be yes. Every Practical Prayer begins with the recognition of a single Creative Power – one Love/Intelligence that creates everything and has done so since the beginning of time. Call it God, Spirit, Christ, Lord, Brahman, Allah, or Nature – it's the One Power in back of everything. We then recognize our connection with this Power, and accept that we use the same creative power to create our lives.

There's one mind, so the idea of "my mind" and "your mind" and "her mind" is a very limited view that can only be held from the perspective of our physical separateness. The effectiveness of Practical Prayer is based on the foundational notion that we're all connected – we're all One. The apparent separation is an illusion of our senses and is what our prayer is intended to supersede.

Prayer for others can be very powerful and highly effective. Our lives are created by beliefs. It can be much easier for another person to have a belief about your good than for you to dig past old wounds and criticism and hidden beliefs to create a new belief for yourself.

Two key factors come into play when we pray for other people. First and foremost, we must be very clear that we are praying for the other person's highest and best. Not what we want for them, but what they want for themselves. Even if you think you know what they want, ask them first.

There's a story of a village elder who was very ill. The loving neighbors cherished him and prayed for his health and survival. He was tired and was ready to let go of life and move on. The prayers resulted in extra weeks of discomfort before he finally passed. In hindsight, a prayer for healing and harmony for the elder and all of the villagers would have been more appropriate.

The factor with the most influence is the belief held by the person being prayed for. Each person will tend to experience their life according to their beliefs, regardless of what you or someone else believes or prays for. It is possible to create a temporary change or healing, but a long-lasting effect is always the result of a change in the person's belief.

Anyone can pray at any time to know that some specific person is an expression of Love, because there is only Love. You can always pray for someone to experience his or her highest and best, because their "highest and best" is within the framework of their own beliefs. You can engage in dialog with someone to get an understanding of his or her inner beliefs. If they're open to the possibility of something better, you have an opportunity for prayer and can help create a new experience for them.

There are professional practitioners of Healing Prayer[‡] who have been trained in the techniques of prayer for others. They work with clients to understand or uncover the beliefs that could be causing an undesirable experience and then pray for a new experience based on a healthier belief.

[‡] Links to Healing Prayer professionals and training organizations can be found at www.be-the-light.com

Scientific Prayer

Practical Prayer is based on the foundational idea that there is One Creative Power in the Universe – one Creator that created and continues to create everything – one Infinite Mind that knows everything. Since everything in the Universe is part of this One, and every individual mind is part of the One Infinite Mind, all knowledge can be accessible anywhere, to anyone. Our connection to the Infinite Mind shows up as intuition, insight, the feeling that something important is happening to someone you care about, premonitions, thinking about a friend right before they call, and all sorts of other mystical experiences.

Practical Prayer is scientific because it is based on a Universal principle. It works all the time, everywhere for everyone, just like gravity or electricity or thermodynamics. Practical Prayer does not require outside approval or authorization. It works all the time, for everyone, whether they realize it or not. As with electricity, study and practice are very helpful in becoming adept in the application of principle. Master electricians are more likely to get the results that they desire than someone who randomly touches bare wires, but the electricity is always working the same way for everyone.

A Paradox: Double Blind Research in a Universe of Oneness

Knowing that we are all connected at a level deeper than our conscious awareness undermines the idea of a rigorous double blind scientific study. The Scientific Method requires that the subject of an experiment be isolated from being influenced by the experimenter. In a medical trial, the subject is given a medication or a placebo by a technician with no knowledge of which it is. The scientists running the experiment have no direct connection with the subjects, and the results of the experiment are considered to be untainted.

When we understand that we are all connected as part of one Universal Mind, and that all knowledge is accessible to anyone, it's easy to see that there's really no such thing as randomness or double blind or untainted results.

So why has this method been so successful? New Thought says the process works because each of the people participating in it *believes* that it works. The subject believes that their illness might be cured. The scientist believes that the therapy could be effective, and the other participants in the process believe that this is a reliable methodology for doing important work. Some of the subjects are cured by the trial therapy and some are not. Some are cured by the placebo, which should not have any physical effect. In fact, drug researchers include response to the placebo effect when categorizing and evaluating the trial results. This is powerful evidence that there is more going on than the medical effects of the compound or procedures being tested by the experimenters.

The cure efected by a placebo and the healing that result from practical prayer are different descriptions of the same process.

A Personal Story of "Miraculous" Healing

For many years I had suffered from a heel spur – a nagging inflammation in my foot that would periodically flare up, making it difficult to walk. My podiatrist, Dr. Brian Goldstein, explained to me that the spur was the sharply pointed end of the bone at the bottom of my heel, which would injure the plantar fascia tendon connecting the heel to the toes.

He offered surgery to correct the problem, and told me that the recuperation would require that I stay off of that foot for six weeks. In further discussion, he explained that many doctors had been successful by making a superficial incision in the skin without cutting the bone or tendon. With six weeks of rest, the patients had about the same results as the ones with surgery. We agreed that, if I had six weeks to invest, I could get similar results without any surgery at all.

Shortly after that, I jumped into the pool with my daughter and her friend. I did not realize that they were kneeling in very shallow water, and hit my heel hard on the concrete bottom of the pool. The pain was excruciating. The next day, Dr. Goldstein told me that it didn't look broken. He took x-rays to be sure, but didn't have time to review them until the following afternoon. By then, my foot felt much better, so I was confident that he'd see nothing on the films. It turned out that I had broken off the heel spur. No surgery required and after hobbling about for a couple of days, I had no further problems.

People envy others
because they do not understand
that there is an unlimited supply
of happiness, love, peace, joy,
ideas, creativity and the like.

Conclusion

"It is done as you believe"

In New Thought, we believe that there is One Creative Power in the Universe that creates everything - including each of us. We further believe that we each use this same Creative Power to create our life. Virtually all of the world's great religions and spiritual practices incorporate the same premise, that we each create our experience according to our beliefs.

The Buddha said, "All that we are is the result of what we have thought. We are made of our thoughts; we are molded by our thoughts". According to Jesus in Mark 11:24, "Whatsoever you desire, believe you have it, and it shall be added unto you". The Bhagavad-Gita (7:21-22) carries the same message, "when a person is devoted to something with complete faith, I unify his faith in that. Then, when faith is completely unified, one gains the object of all devotion. In this way, every desire is fulfilled by me."

Practical Prayer is a specific technique to help us understand, refine and define our beliefs and thereby create real results in our lives. There is no magic to it, and the technique can be used by anyone of any religion, or no religion at all. The key is to do it. Stop thinking about it, stop studying it and trying to understand how it could possibly work. Pray for something. It almost doesn't matter what you pray for, as long as it's positive, present tense, and life affirming.

A Practical Prayer for something that feels inconsequential is a great way to get started. Pray for an unexpected contact from an old friend, or green lights while you're driving, or parking spaces close to the door. Pick something that you don't have any hidden beliefs about, something that could happen to you "by coincidence," and see what happens. The proof of your prayer's effectiveness is in the results. The old saying that "I'll believe it when I see it" is exactly backwards. It's when we believe something – really believe it – that we'll see it in our lives.

Your word is the power
you have to create.

Appendix – The Steps of Practical Prayer explained

Recognition (God Is)

In this crucial First Step, you turn your attention to the spiritual nature of the Universe in which we all live. Turn away from the physical world that surrounds you, even if that's where you want to see the change. As an example, if you want to change your living room, you can either start pushing furniture around or take a quiet moment to think about what you want to create. You could even call in a designer. In this first Recognition step, you look beyond current circumstances and connect with the Creator. Recognize the Unity of all that is and release any thoughts of duality or inherent conflict. You call on the Designer.

This is your Recognition of the divine qualities of God, or Infinite Mind, or the One Universal Intelligence. It doesn't matter how you frame the concept, as long as you're connecting with your own understanding of the One creative power that brought everything we know of into existence. Focus on the qualities or aspects that correspond to the area in which you want to experience change.

The universal aspects of God are Abundance, Balance, Beauty, Creativity, Energy, Freedom, Goodness, Harmony, Intelligence, Joy, Life, Love, Oneness, Order, Peace, Power, Strength, Truth, Unity, and Wholeness. Choose one (or more) that support the result that you're prayer is intended to achieve.

The Recognition step is complete when your awareness and attention are on the infinite power and potential existing throughout the Universe.

 Unification (I Am)

Next, turn your attention to your involvement and participation in this creative Universe. With the understanding that God is all there is, that God is everywhere, God is everyone and everything, acknowledge that HAS TO include you. It includes *everything*. There is no possibility that God is everywhere EXCEPT the three feet around you.

With this awareness, acknowledge the qualities or aspects of God that you recognized in the first step are also available and accessible to you. Because God is within and all around you, these attributes and possibilities are within you, too.

I like to think of this as acknowledging that we're on the A-team. Speaking an affirmation, especially for something desirable and important that we don't currently have in our life experience, can feel small and powerless. When we precede the affirmation by remembering that we're on the team with God, the affirmation tends to feel much more powerful.

The Unification step is complete when you feel a personal connection to the infinite power and potential existing throughout the Universe, knowing they are available to and present in you.

Appendix – The Steps of Practical Prayer explained

❗ Realization or Affirmation (I Know)

This is a statement of the good that you're claiming. It's a life-affirming statement that's powerful, positive, personal, and present tense. Your affirmation must be truthful and believable to you.

We use words of Truth in our affirmations, even if the situation we're claiming doesn't currently exist for us. This can seem tricky, but once you understand the concept, it becomes simple. An example might be a student worried about an exam, fearful of being unprepared and getting an unsatisfactory grade. An affirmation of "I get an A on the test" is not truthful – it's wishful thinking. That affirmation might go beyond her believability and could trigger a bunch of "yeah-but" objections in her mind. Instead, the affirmation could be, "I know there are 50 questions on the exam, and I have studied and learned well in excess of fifty answers. I know I have the perfect answer for every question on the exam".

The affirmation must fit into the belief system of the one doing the praying and the one being prayed for. It is a way of creating a new belief, but cannot simply be layered on top of an existing belief. The affirmation must be truthful and believable; something that is already true or could be true to the individuals involved.

It's possible that you're claiming something that simply isn't true. On these rare occasions you'll usually feel awkwardness about the claim you're making. When this happens you can step back to the affirmation and fine-tune the idea or the language you're using to make the statement both true and believable to you. An overweight man looking to shed extra pounds might get a "yeah-but" from claiming, "I weigh 160 pounds". He could then revise the affirmation to "my weight is now dropping easily, quickly, and comfortably to 160 pounds". When this new statement resonates as truthful and believable, the affirmation is complete.

 ## Gratitude (I am Grateful)

Having claimed your good (and gotten any conflicting notions out of the way) give thanks for the good. Feel as if you already have it and express gratitude for the good, for the giving nature of God, for your ability to create your life experience, for your awareness of your connection with God.

Gratitude is a confirmation of your openness and acceptance for the good that's in your life and on the way. It is also an expression of humility. This is crucial once you become adept at using Practical Prayer to create new and joyous experiences in your life. The results of successful prayers can be quite a thrill – a great job, new friends, a sports car – and lots of people find that their ego can chime in to claim credit for being good at creating stuff through prayer. Gratitude is a humbling expression, acknowledging that the good is coming through you and counteracts any ego-driven or self-centered notion that the good is coming from you.

In the gratitude step, turn your attention once again to the Infinite Power that creates everything and for your ability to participate in creating with it.

Release (I let it go)

Practical Prayer is not about willing something to happen, or holding an idea in mind. Once you've arrived at a new understanding of the good that's at hand, get out of the way. When a gardener plants a seed in rich soil where it will be tended and watered, he doesn't dig up the seed to see if it's germinating properly. The same is true with a prayer. Speak your creative Word, release it to the Law, and let the Law take it from there. God said "Let there be Light," and there was Light. God did not go back to check that it was bright enough or to change the bulb. The Law responded as it always does, with a loud, resounding "YES", and there was Light.

Refutation and Re-affirmation (The "yeah-buts")

Your Affirmation is a statement of Truth, your new belief about the situation or circumstance about which you're praying. As soon as the Affirmation feels right, you move on to the Gratitude step and let it go. When it doesn't feel believable to you, when an objection or resistance comes to mind, you're uncovering a hidden belief. This hidden belief has no more truth or power than anything else and in fact could be a false belief lurking in the shadows of your mind. The objection often feels like a little voice arguing with the claim you're making, saying something like, "yeah, but that's not true," or "yeah, but you're not good enough," "you're not lovable enough," "you're not important enough," "you don't deserve this good," or "you've only failed in this area in the past." Your negative self-talk can be very creative.

When a "yeah-but" comes up, bring it out into the open and meet it head on. You have already established that the Good you're claiming exists in the Universe and that it's available to you. Now you can turn the negativity of your false belief back on itself by saying something along the lines of, "any idea that this good is not available to me is simply untrue," or "the thought that I somehow don't deserve this good is a fabrication and returns to the murky shadows from which it crept," or "the Love that exists everywhere in the Universe doesn't stop in the three feet around me." Use the attributes of God and your connection with that infinite power to counter any false beliefs that come up. You're an A-Team player, and there's no room for a limiting, bush-league idea to dictate your life.

The Refutation is always followed by a Re-affirmation. It can be exactly the same as the initial affirmation or can be adjusted or re-worded to more fully resonate as both truthful and believable. If another "yeah-but" comes up, repeat the Refutation and Re-affirmation. Continue this cycle as long as necessary until you've achieved clarity that your statements are truthful and believable to you and then move on to the Gratitude step.

Appendix – The Steps of Practical Prayer explained

God can do no more for you
than God can do through you.

Bonus: A Prayer of Thanksgiving

There is One Power and Presence forever sharing Itself as every part of life. A limitless Source of Good, always giving of Itself as Its creation, revealing Its nature in the Abundance present everywhere. It is the Eternal Gift emerging into our lives.

Each of us is some part of this Eternal Gift, a unique idea in the Mind of Spirit, embodying and living this experience.

I claim the good of Prosperity, Love, Joy, and Peace in this time of Thanksgiving. I know that this Good is right here, right now. This is the Eternal Gift of life and some part of this Gift is here to celebrate in each of our lives at this moment. The One Power is the Limitless Source of Good and each one here is the same Good. The One Power is Love and so is each of us. The One Power is Whole and so we are complete. The One Power is Unity and so we are all together in life.

We give thanks for the Good we receive and the Good that we give, for the Love that we share, for the Joys we experience, and for the Peace that we are. We celebrate this life in all Its wonder as we give thanks for our Good.

And so, knowing that this Good is now present as and through and around each one, I release this word to Spirit knowing that Spirit has already responded with a resounding YES!

And so it is

Bringing a wonderful, delightful new life
into the world can be a painful process.
The same can apply to a New Thought.

About the Author

Rev. Bill Marchiony is Co-Founder and Spiritual Director of New Thought Philadelphia, a community dedicated to individual growth through Spirit, self and service. He and his group recognize the divinity in each person, and support one another in a deepening awareness that we each have the authority & accountability to create our lives and our experience as we believe, through intention and love.

New Thought Philadelphia is online at:
>   www.NewThoughtPhilly.org.

Bill's spiritual studies began in 1996; he's been a Religious Science Practitioner since 2002, and received ministerial credentials from the Emerson Theological Institute in 2011. Rev. Bill has been a Teen Group advisor and leader since 2005, and founded the Northeast Regional Teen program which has grown to include more than 150 participants in twenty Centers reaching from Washington, DC to Albany, NY.

By day Bill runs First Name Basis, a cross-media marketing company. In the way-distant past he was a "zany" morning radio personality in Philadelphia, Charleston, SC and Miami, FL.

Purpose: _____

※ _____
_____
_____
_____
_____

🕊 _____
_____
_____
_____
_____
_____
_____
_____

! _____
_____
_____
_____
_____
_____
_____

Worksheet for Your Own Prayer

?

!!

🧘

🧍

And so it is!

Practical Prayer for Real Results

Purpose: _____

Worksheet for Your Own Prayer

? _____

!! _____

 _____

 _____

And so it is!

Purpose: _____

Worksheet for Your Own Prayer

? _____

!! _____

_____

_____

And so it is!

Purpose: _____

※ _____

🧍 _____

! _____

Worksheet for Your Own Prayer

? _____

!! _____

🙇 _____

🧍 _____

And so it is!

Practical Prayer for Real Results

Purpose: _____

Worksheet for Your Own Prayer

?

!!

🙇

🧍

And so it is!

Purpose: _____

Worksheet for Your Own Prayer

? _____

!! _____

🧘 _____

🧍 _____

And so it is!

Purpose: _____

※ _____

🕊 _____

! _____

Worksheet for Your Own Prayer

? _____

_____

_____

_____

‼ _____

_____

_____

_____

_____

_____

🧎 _____

_____

_____

_____

_____

🕴 _____

_____

_____

And so it is!

Made in the USA
Middletown, DE
24 December 2017